The Spiritual Life

Psychic Protection on the Internal Journey

John Stone

Cover Art by Judith Shaw:

Guardians of the Passage

For all those seeking

the Internal Life

Other Books by John Stone

Gifts from Above, How Spirit heals us during Illness

Cultivating the Divine, Healing the Dark Masculine – Book I in the Dream Trilogy

Faeries Found, a guide to entering the Faerie Realms

Daring to Dream, a guide to Lucid Dreaming, Astral Travel and Spiritual Growth

The King of Camelot, a dreamer's account of the life of King Arthur

Future Books

Dream Trilogy, Books II and III

Acknowledgements

It is long past time that I gave thanks to Marilynn, a good friend that helped get me started on this path many years ago. With Gratitude...

Table of Contents

The Internal Life

At some point during our life on the Earth, whether delivered through trauma, loss, illness, or simply the arrival of Divine inspiration, many of us will long to remember something buried deep within. Forgotten for a time, our innate ability to see, feel, and know from the spiritual perspective, eventually wins over our awareness. Gradually or suddenly, our inner life can unexpectedly become as important as physical existence. As on some level we know that our outer life is transient, impermanent, and is first created within. Seeds to life and love require planting and must be tended if we are to create the life of dreams. And it all begins in the internal world...

For most of us, accessing the internal world requires that we slow down our external life, at least to the point that living becomes more manageable. When our external life remains busy, our thoughts remain fixed there. We are grounded in the physical dimension. In slowing down, we naturally become more reflective. Our thoughts move inward toward unresolved conflicts or perhaps seek answers to deeper spiritual questions. It is there that we are confronted with our conscience, uncertainties, and dormant dreams. And that means feeling the fear that exists within.

It also causes us to face the knowledge that we are powerful and that we have greater capacities for living than we know. An internal life gives us the opportunity to draw from a deeper guidance and live by a higher set of laws.

It does take courage to stop and see, to be willing to know ourselves as we truly are, to know what motivates and inspires us, as well as what limits us. It is much easier to separate from the deeper levels of feeling, and to focus our thoughts in a shallow perspective. At least in the short term, that allows us to separate from our feeling body, where we must face the rejection of others...

As a young child, I often had night time dream experiences that rivaled the consciousness I had when awake. Sometimes even confusing my dream experiences with my daytime activities, I couldn't always differentiate between the two. Powerful dream consciousness was a gift that disappeared in my teenage years, but even so, never completely left my awareness. Its memory always remained in the back of my mind.

Gratefully, the return of my dream awareness was destined to return later in life, and when I began seeking a conscious spiritual life, a fascination with spiritual dreams dominated my thoughts. As I grew in awareness of spirit, the consciousness within my dream experiences also expanded.

I didn't discover an instant ability to travel in my dreams—I was gradually introduced to those realms. And interestingly, the most profound aspect of my dreams was not always the experiences themselves, but of the consciousness *attained* within them.

After my skill in dream travel had developed, I would estimate that my ability to *feel* during travels, would increase a minimum of twenty, or perhaps even thirty times or more. It was like being deeply dipped into my being, allowing me to experience a wholeness of spirit that had never even reached my imagination. So intensely profound, I could only maintain those feelings for a few moments after waking, before my awakened state consciousness overpowered them. My ego would then numb my body's ability to feel, in order to cope with the pressures in my day to day life.

But even though I could no longer feel to the same depth during the day as compared to the night, I could still remember that I had the ability to do so. And I would be left wondering throughout the day, how can I reach that level of Oneness again? How can I bring those feelings, that clarity and knowing into my conscious awake state?

With my body sound asleep, and my soul body experiencing the dream world, I found myself sitting in a classroom, in the *Conscious Awake School*. This was one of my first out of body experiences, before I had developed a lot of consciousness in the dream worlds. I was barely aware in this realm and all of my prior experiences in this class had remained in my subconscious. But this night, as a result of the teachings given to us in this classroom to develop more consciousness, I was awakening. I had turned a dream that would normally remain in my subconscious, into an experience that would lead me toward the gradual awareness of my true nature.

When I awoke that morning, the memory followed into my consciousness. I now knew without a doubt, that I was being assisted.

After a few out of body experiences, coping with my physical life actually seemed to become a little more difficult. I was experiencing a life of extreme opposites. In the night, if fortunate enough to have a conscious dream, I would experience an indescribable wholeness. Then upon waking, I'd shift to the opposite end of that spectrum, to experience the complete void of an internal world. It was very distressing.

But the seed had been planted and I could not now turn back. Forward was the only direction, and I continued to *unconsciously* seek the development of my internal life…

I've already written many books and articles about how to develop these dreaming abilities, so that is not the purpose of this book. I will jump ahead now. But what had begun as an occasional lucid dream or out of body experience, perhaps one every three or four months, eventually turned into almost nightly travel. This presented a new set of problems. Having this much consciousness in realms that had shortly before been unconscious, caused me to face many situations that I did not understand. It also opened me up to a new set of friends, entities in spirit not presently incarnated but with a connection to me from the past, from prior lives and existences.

Many were positive, uplifting and inspirational beyond description. Others were encounters that tested me to my core. Challenges came from less evolved beings that might be connected to me from a shared past life in the Earth, or other lower forms of life.

While the encounters with the higher forms of life were not threatening, I began to find challenge from some of the lower entities. And with my physical life frustrating me, I was creating a lot of negative energy in my aura, and for a time they were able to pull me down into their frequency of thought. And that is the purpose of this book, to describe some of my encounters, and to explain how psychic protection is both won and lost.

Encountering Darkness

The Hero and Fool, each standing on opposite ends of the polar spectrum, need each other to survive. Without the energy from its opposite and complementing frequency, both exist without balance. Both seek each other's company, and both are subject to psychic assault—*without the other.*

The spiritual adept however, manages both of these aspects completely within themselves. When stepping out of balance, the spiritually attuned simply finds the knowledge and power that will restore balance, completely within themselves. They are their own Hero. You might be able to imagine the resulting psychic protection, if you do not experience life in this way. There is no dependency on another for protection. No one wishes you harm…

The polar opposite of any vibration of frequency is going to be magnetic to its opposite. It is spiritual law. If our thinking is that we are better than another person, we are vibrating in a frequency that is going to attract conflict from the object of our judgment. We do not have to say a word. We will simply magnetize a person or situation to show us that we have more in common with the focus of our disdain than we realize.

In addition to that, we will similarly be having multiple experiences in simultaneous, alternate spiritual dimensions for the purpose of accelerating this release. In these other dimensions, we may be experiencing more serious repercussions to our energetic infractions than we might experience in the physical realm. This is the purpose of being incarnated into a realm of multiple dimensions. It allows us to experience and intuitively grow in knowledge without having to fully feel all of the energetic assault that might result from our thinking.

For instance, if we were to tell someone uninvited, their way of life was incorrect, or if we confronted them even more forcefully in the physical realm, we have to face the conflict we created. We might receive a verbal assault or perhaps a physical one. But when acting out in alternate dimensions, the learning is intuitively passed down to the physical presence, without consciously receiving all of the conflict. Of course many still act out in the physical realm and magnetize great amounts of emotional, psychic, and physical violence to manifest in their lives. But I would suggest that these people are creating even more desperate acts of violence in the spiritual dimensions.

When trying to resolve conflict in one's life, it's easy to imagine a world in which no one challenges us. We might even spend time day dreaming of being so powerful that everyone leaves us alone to do as we please. I would suggest, that this is not truly what we are seeking, that we are instead—seeking a *sense* of control.

When first waking in a conscious dream experience, we are most often, if the dream work was prepared with the assistance of our higher power, going to awaken in a dimension within ourselves.

I liken it to being in one's room when a child. It's our room. We can do anything we want there. Hang a picture on the wall, rearrange furniture, and perhaps even change the color of the room, with the help of our parents.

Now when walking out of our room and into the hall, we must open to a new set of laws. Brothers and sisters suddenly have more influence in our lives. Walking further into our home and into the living room, a completely new set of rules exist. We are entering co-creative zones. Let us take it even further and walk outside and down the street. We are then opening up our world and having to face the agreed upon limits by our co-creative partners—our neighbors.

The further we get from our personal space, the less power we may feel. These principles work similarly when opening up in the internal worlds. So we are slowly introduced to the greater Universe at large, and for good reason. It is no different than first attending kindergarten before elementary school, then Junior High before High School and College. We must gradually understand the forces we are facing so that our body may acclimate to the intensity of the energies.

But ultimately we learn. And it usually first requires the passage and experience of many lives—that we are not seeking control over others—but a *sense* of control in our world, control over *ourselves*.

When we reach this place of internal power, we find peace within ourselves, and are no longer *only* protected by the physical laws established in the Earth. A new set of higher laws arrive that offer a different and much more expansive level of protection.

Establishing Communication

One afternoon while napping on the couch, the image of a single horizontal line appear in my mind. With my consciousness drifting somewhere between a hazy dream and slightly awake, I had yet to realize what was happening. But slowly the width of the line began to change, to waver, and soon appear as if a sine wave on an oscilloscope identifying sound. As the line continued its rhythmic, enchanting dance, sound was gradually and gently added. Slowly becoming more recognizable, I could eventually hear a voice accompany the dancing image—spirit communication. Shocked back into a fully awake state, I was overwhelmed by my surprise.

This was the first time that I had ever heard an entity directly speak to me in an altered, but higher state of consciousness. It wasn't a hazy dream, where I was much more comfortable receiving impressions, images and messages. By the end of the experience, I was bordering on full consciousness.

It was of course, very exciting and I immediately imagined the possibilities. I believed that my guides would soon be able to directly speak to me, reciting great wisdom that would eliminate all of the uncertainties and frustrations from my life. What else might I imagine? But things didn't go as planned. What I hadn't yet understood, was that this was barely a beginning. I was just now stepping onto the path of transcending the Earth's physical dimension—and I was about to be both challenged and rewarded.

White Eagle, as channeled by Grace Cooke suggests, the quicker one can hear their own personal voice of conscience, the quicker one will travel the road towards this type of hearing on the inner plane, and to experience *clairaudience*.

The frequencies of thought emanating from those in spirit (that are malevolent beings) are usually just minimally higher in frequency than those incarnated in the physical Earth. This means that when tuning our hearing to the next level up, the ones we may hear, at least at first can sometimes be entities of lower consciousness. It requires additional spiritual purification, provided by a spiritual practice to reach higher beings. So initially we can be tested, just as Jesus once described, by first hearing less evolved beings offering temptation.

Several weeks later, I was again taking a nap on the couch. Drifting near the edge of consciousness, I hadn't yet fallen asleep when an image popped into my mind. I was clearly seeing the partially extended wing of a falcon or bird of prey. The feathers however, were not their typical colors. These were various shades of blue.

The wing itself took up most of the space in my mind, so I could see nothing else, until it abruptly disappeared and was replaced by the image of an old druid.

"Can you do this?" he sharply stated.

"*Ahhhhhh*," I yelled out loud, as my body jumped. Instantly raising into a sitting position, I tried to pull myself together after experiencing such shock.

I sat there almost cross eyed as I began to more fully awaken. Then, I began to consider the meaning of the image. This was my first direct *contact* with an entity while experiencing a high degree of consciousness in an altered state.

I would ponder the experience for years...

When talking about communicating with spirits, a friend once mentioned *energy signature*, while referring to the feelings you feel about an entity when speaking to them. My countenance sparked, "Yes, exactly."

Every entity and incarnated person, always has an energy signature. The challenge being that, particularly in the physical dimension, people can often mask that to a great degree.

Many of the Earth's darkest leaders could mask the feelings around their voice and appear to be benevolent souls. But it is much harder to do in the higher spiritual dimensions, as more facets of one's being are exposed. And with our own egos being dramatically diminished in these realms, we have the ability to feel to much deeper levels. So we have greater access to (feel) the levels of conflict and incongruence within another soul.

Souls are limited by their own internal peace. Their limit being which dimensions that they can enter and exist within. One with emotional violence within is going to be limited close to the coarser Earth dimensions in their travel. This is why darker thoughts have the least amount of power and influence in the greater Universe. Those frequencies can only travel in resonant dimensions and will not leave the vicinity of the Earth's lower dimensions. This is how order exists in the Universe.

I've met thousands beings in out of body travels and visions, and I find that entities have an infinite number of variations of evolution. Some have great experience and knowledge while others are very young souls, and it can initially be difficult to discern the difference. Without the heavy ego they would have if incarnated into the Earth, it is much easier for an entity to appear more dynamic in personality in spirit realms.

But I have found in general, the more talkative, self-assured and in control one appears, the less likely they are to being highly evolved.

A highly evolved being will be able to change the energy around your being and lift you in consciousness without uttering a single word. Whereas a young soul will instead need to make promises and offer something tangible to gain your attentions. They may make assurances about a specific outcome in the future or outline actions for you to achieve a goal. I always treat such advice with the caution.

While an evolved soul might in fact give you a glimpse of the future in certain situations, or comfort you by occasionally revealing an outcome, it is never done casually. When these events occur, it is done with a lot of consideration by God and the beings that oversee your life. I always assume one that regularly gives such counsel cannot be trusted. And I have come to this conclusion by experience, by simply seeing their promises repeatedly fail.

Divine law prevents anyone from passing on more knowledge to those in the Earth, than they are able to receive.

We can however, feel desperate enough that we might believe we just *have* to have an answer to a question, *before we are truly ready to hear it.* This opens a door to the lower world and enables beings of a lower vibration to communicate with us. For this reason, patience is very important when following a spiritual path.

There are many layers and levels of truth. So any being that would share more than we are able to receive, originates from a lower level of consciousness. And any being that answers every question that we ask, is unlikely providing answers from the highest sources.

Being open to such an entity, our thoughts begin to mix with theirs allowing lustful energies to enter our aura and create even more confusion. For most people, this simply just results in states of uncertainty, anxiety, or panic.

For the reasons outlined above, it is very important to be satisfied with the communications that we receive, understanding that what is now a cryptic message, may later on become very clear. It's about Trust. We are wishing to establish soulful communication with spirit realms, things that nourish us on a deep level. And answering every question of the ego does not hold great importance for the soul, nor create depth.

When we can exist in this state of trust, we are maintaining a doorway to the highest energies of thought. Because it can take years to resolve certain issues regarding our lives, the world of spirit goes about planting seeds. And like any seed planted in the Earth's soil, it takes time to mature and grow. Insisting on details is resistance. If what we are given is from the highest sources and truth, in time the knowledge will bear fruit, will be understood. I always trust answers more that are intuited over a long period of time.

But benevolent beings *can* tell you many things, when you have already begun to understand the answer. That is because receiving the answer is not going to overwhelm or violate your energy. By helping you to understand in this way, they would only be quickening the answer inside of yourself.

It is also good to be cautious of answers that come from within in a specific dimension, even from a benevolent source. They may only be appropriate in that dimensional space. In other words, that answer may only apply to your experience in the reality in which it was given and not be appropriate for your physical life. So it is important when considering advice given, "Does it truly apply to my physical life?" Making quick assumptions regarding communications, can cause confusion. I always carefully consider any guidance before implementing physical action.

Visions

Visions, those fleeting images that arrive in the mind, are offered to us from the world of spirit in guidance and to establish clarity. Contrary to some schools of thought, I do not believe these images are necessarily meant to prophetically lead us. Some of the visions I receive, in fact, are things I do not wish to happen.

I believe that visions arrive to help us make choices, by allowing us to see potential outcomes before they are physically manifested. And that, as most people might imagine, is a great gift. It's easily as important to know what we *do not* want, as to know what we *want*.

A vision can give us a sense and feel of a potential future, to assist us in our contemplation of future choices. I have many times thought I wanted something to arrive in my life, only to experience it in a vision and decide otherwise. And as I became more comfortable in receiving visions, more layers arrived. They were no longer merely images, but became multi-leveled experiences of feeling that would help me to intuit my interest in their manifestation.

Most people really have no idea of the degree of communication that exists, the varied exchanges of energy and thought that occurs between two people when meeting. Images are unconsciously exchanged during discussion that help us to understand each other. These are also visions, though from a different source—other people.

Entities in spirit can also share similar visions when meeting you or just thinking of you. So these images, *visions*, can arrive from multiple sources. And if that is the case, it is easy to see why no assumptions should be made concerning their meaning.

I am very open to receiving visions, and that is because I try not to attach to their outcome. I don't act in a way to bring the vision into the physical, but instead, simply prepare in case it were to arrive. That way, I am able to keep a certain distance from them, a comfort zone while I contemplate and interpret their meaning. This enables them to easily enter my conscious mind. And that's because I realize I have some degree of control over their manifestation.

Visions can only come from sources resonant with our current vibrational frequency. This is how the door to the visionary world is guarded. It's physics. So the quality of any vision, will be directly related to the purity of one's soul, and specifically to the amount of fear one is currently experiencing in their lives. And our body's vibrational frequency is not sourced so much by conscious fear, as it is by unconscious fear. Our collective fear then gives entrance to those resonating frequencies of energy, originating from varied sources.

An unevolved being in spirit can easily share a vision with us, if we are open to their frequency of thought.

During this present cycle in the Earth's evolution, we can find affirmation for anything we desire. Good or bad, we can find resonant energy to agree with our position in life. From doing volunteer work, to robbing a bank, we can find support. We are fortunate that God will often intervene when we desire something that is not good for us. But when our soul is sufficiently magnetic to an unpleasant event, God often allows the experience to come to pass. This is so that we may learn from the experience and no longer maintain the magnetic connection to it in the future.

These are great reasons to carefully consider all images that arrive from the visionary world, in order to help make sure any resulting manifestations are appropriate.

The Power of Prayer

I remember as a young child looking at a shadow box on the wall in our church's Parish Hall. In it, was a pamphlet that read, *How to Pray.*

An almost threatening title, it completely grabbed my attention for months. I innately knew that this topic held great importance for my life. But I never had the courage to take a copy for myself, or even to just take it down and read it.

My family went to church most Sundays and I had attended numerous Sunday School classes. I listened to many priests talk about prayer, yet in my soul, I was not satisfied with the knowledge I had so far received.

But when one begins to see into the internal worlds, it is difficult not to grow in understanding of the power of prayer. We see that the happenings in spirit are overpowering in scale when compared to life in the physical Earth. Life, dreams, healing and hope all reside in their fullest form in the higher worlds. And it is up to us to draw that energy down into this dimension, to first enrich our own lives—and ultimately the planet and all of its lifeforms.

At this point I do not think I need to make a further case for adding prayer into one spiritual practice. Many very well know of the benefits. But as I have grown in my knowledge of the inner worlds, I have come to realize that a higher power truly does have things in hand. And particularly that my own needs or wants, might not always be the best thing for myself or for recipients of my prayer.

There are also energetic consequences to attachment in any form. So for the sake of maintaining a close connection to God, and avoiding negative energetic consequences, I choose to defer to God's will in prayer. And I do that by avoiding requests for specific outcomes.

Since I have discovered that I am not always able to see the highest potential outcome for myself or those in my prayers, I usually have a very simple request, asking just for *divine guidance*.

I have found that the resulting gifts, are usually much better than I had hoped for...

Divine Protection

It's very interesting to me how the Universe uses those in our lives to help us. A very high percentage of the people that I have known in the physical, and have since passed into the world of spirit, still return on occasion to help me understand lessons and teach me about the world.

Dean was once my best friend in Elementary school. Even though we moved in different directions as we grew up, and that he passed away while I was in my twenties, he still returns to be involved in some of my lessons.

While I never saw Dean harm anyone or even put someone down, people seemed to think negatively of him. He was considered a shadowy character, in part because he just didn't care about excelling in school. It is unfortunate that he would receive that level of judgement in the Earth, as his actual reality is quite different. In spirit, he is somewhat priest-like.

Sharing a lucid dream experience with him, we were standing near the shore of a lake. We had been out on the water in a canoe-like boat and had just jumped onto the shore. But now the boat was beginning to drift away. In order to prevent losing it, Dean jumped back on board. Remarkably, the inertia from him landing in the bow did not push the boat further away. Instead, the boat immediately began moving back toward shore, opposing the force that had just been placed upon it. Having my fully awake state consciousness in this experience and believing in the normally accepted limitations of the physical Earth, I was completely amazed. Witnessing this with such lucidity was a little overwhelming.

But what I next saw would later be realized as one of the most important experiences ever witnessed in travel.

After he secured the boat and we began walking up the shore, I could see Dean's thoughts as they emanated from his mind. As if he were a cartoon character, a little bubble appeared above his head that was full of words. I could literally read each sentence. And the thoughts emanating were about God. As if in a continual state of prayer, he was surrounded with the protective energy of God.

In the future days ahead, I often returned in thought to this experience and why it was offered to me. It would take months of contemplation, but I eventually saw the amazing benefits of protection this affords, if one's life is lived with a similar focus. When focused on what God would give us, rather than what our ego might desire, a very stabilizing balance enters our life. Our choices become slightly different and our sense of timing more acute. We develop additional patience, and that translates into a deeper gratitude for the gifts we receive.

While there are many aspects to psychic protection, there is one important overriding factor—karma. There is no event that occurs during our life that is forgotten. If we do something that energetically harms another, we will suffer that same energetic consequence ourselves. We reap what we sow.

This is perhaps one of the greatest reasons why as a culture, the Western World resists an internal focus. We have guilt inside. And becoming internally focused, requires us to face all of that guilt.

While I believe it is important to take the time required to transmute the energetic infractions we commit in our lives, I also find compassion for myself and others for the mistakes we have made. With the world's great darkness bearing down upon us, it is very easy to withhold—to look the other way when we could have offered help. Or to say or do something unkind that was unnecessary.

And we really are not given the tools to understand that errors are not condemning. If we just can find the trust within ourselves to look at the past with forgiving eyes, we set into motion energy to correct our errors. We are also given opportunities in alternate dimensions to amend our mistakes, so we are not always required to make physical reparations. The change in our thinking, is sometimes enough repair the fabric of our errors.

But when one is able to look into the eye of conscience, be willing to see their own darkness and fault, a new level of protection exists. This is because instead of resisting the surrounding energies, we are uniting with them, making peace.

While I find that this process can be very difficult, and that facing one's conscience can be a life-long process of realization, it for me has been my greatest liberator. And it is a very difficult thing to do in this age. The race consciousness energy surrounding western culture does not permit this. We are encouraged to stay busy and run from an internal life.

We often believe in the unspoken fears in this world and because of this, must face their resulting limitations. But that fear that propels us into activity, to avoid the internal stillness, is actually the door into these rich inner worlds. We only have to become aware, gently slowing our lives down. We can have very little guidance in our outer world leading us toward these realizations, taking us back to our innate and intuitive powers. But the inner urgings if followed, know the way.

When we follow our intuitive guidance, inner feelings that suggest should we do this or that, we can be divinely led into experiences to neutralize or pay back karma.

Most can hardly even remember a past life, so it is difficult to know of our actions there. But I would suggest that virtually everyone, myself included, have things to pay back, favors to return from those that have helped us along the way. And when following one's intuition, we are able to do this, even if unconsciously. The action is the only thing that is important.

But when we are in this place of balance, in a place of giving back to others, we find the greatest psychic protection. If there is ever a moment where one is confused and does not know what to do with their life, consider an action that gives something to another person. When we give anything from an unconditional space, the consciousness of the entire planet is incrementally lifted.

This is the importance of remaining as present as possible. When we are present, we are more likely to act on those inner urgings. And they can lead us toward activity that returns our wholeness.

Honoring Life

When we reach a certain age, we are forced to face that during our lifetime, we will know people that leave the Earth in untimely deaths. And I have personally had a few friends to pass from this world by their own hands, committing suicide. I have not met every one of them in the astral world, but I have been given access to two friends that took their lives during my earlier years. And each experiences the after-life very differently...

William was a good friend in Elementary School. We often spent recess together in the fourth grade, where he sometimes held court by telling one of his amazingly crafted and completely fictitious stories. We believed every word.

As we grew up, we also grew apart. I wasn't close to him at the time of his passing, but I do remember hearing of his death. It came by word of mouth, drifting from person to person as it was passed along the streets of our neighborhood.

His parents forbade him to see his girlfriend, I heard. And in a moment of rage, he took a gun and pulled the trigger.

As I progressed on my spiritual path, I wondered how he might now be experiencing life. And then one night, he arrived in a dream.

I've never actually sat down and spoken with him directly, as I have done with many of my other friends that have passed. He always appears in the distance. For instance, I might be engaged with another person in a lucid experience when I glance across the room to discover him lurking behind the scenes. Making a funny gesture and trying to make me laugh, he always arrives with a comedic edge. But it's very apparent that he is in good spirits and very happy. Mike on the other hand, did not fare the same.

I've only seen him a couple of times and he's obviously not in a very good place, or at least wasn't during our last meeting. His passing was very different.

He had been depressed before his suicide and had even experienced a failed attempt. I had seen him in the physical a few years before he died and had spoken to him about it. I was very young and unable to offer much comfort.

Mike was likeable, handsome, attractive and an athletic talent. He seemed to have everything going for him. But all those gifts were not enough to help him maintain his balance in the Earth.

When we met in the dream state, his energy had an obvious heaviness to it. He was still *very* depressed, unable to even smile. And this was several years after his passing. It was if I could feel the imploded energy surrounding him, the result of directing such violence toward himself. He was still not free even though being released from the heaviness of the Earth's dense field.

There are many views and opinions about suicide. While I do not see a right or wrong here, I have seen from my visits with Mike, that you do not escape depression and hopelessness from self-inflicted death. That in fact, it appears to worsen the situation. The resulting implosion of energy from a planned suicide actually makes it harder to move through that kind of emotional state—even in the lightness of the spirit world.

William, as far as I know, was never depressed. He hadn't planned his suicide and in a sense, it was a complete mistake. Whereas it was very obvious that Mike had wanted to die for years.

Once when my spiritual teacher Carla was channeling, her guide Mary spoke through on the topic. She said that in suicide, you just bring more difficulty upon yourself. That in fact, you must return to the Earth, and experience life in even more difficult conditions during your next incarnation.

I have great sympathy for any soul enduring such feelings, and can only hope that anyone experiencing that kind of difficulty can reach out to others. It is not possible to want to impose death upon yourself, without being lost in the illusion of the Earth. For if we can get to a place to see the *reality* of the Universe, we find that redemption is always available.

When someone contemplates suicide, leaving the Earth may seem like the perfect solution. But in many cases, I would suggest that we are simply desiring to experience our consciousness more fully, as if we were still in spirit. A part of us remembers existing without the great density and loss of consciousness we must face in the Earth. And we are simply in need of removing the darkness that has gathered within us. But the greater clarity that we remember as spirit, is still available to us.

It can feel like a liberating fantasy to depart, but peace can be found by clearing lower energies from our internal space, from within our aura. When that has been cleansed, we do not feel the heavy weight bearing down upon us – we no longer have the need or desire to leave the planet. This clearing requires regular maintenance to stay above the Earth's illusion, and is the result and purpose of developing a spiritual practice.

Returning Fragments

One of the greatest opportunities that can be realized while deepening one's dream world, is the discovery and healing of the missing pieces of the Self. It is difficult not to accumulate wounds on the way to maturity, and it requires a concerted effort in order to heal them. With each wound that is discovered, a missing fragment of the soul exists. When we are still quite young, these missing pieces begin to manifest as a loss in consciousness. And with every new loss, the totality results in the evaporation of our dream consciousness—we become less and less conscious of our daytime *and* nighttime dreams. Many people stop remembering their dreams altogether.

Along with this fragmentation, the resulting loss of consciousness can cause us to lose the awareness of our own darkness. This knowledge is one of the most important facets of growing dream consciousness, and particularly, in our personal psychic protection in our daily lives and nighttime dream travels. For when we have lost awareness of our darkness, humility, and awareness of a higher power, we have opened a door to receiving a lesson. And that is a lesson to show us that there is in fact, darkness within us.

These fragments of our consciousness can have a life of their own. They express themselves unconsciously through our personality, as well as in dream realms and alternate dimensions. But conflict is certain to arrive when we have lost awareness of our humility. It is for this reason that part of my own spiritual practice is looking for darkness within myself and being open to it existing there. It does.

Darkness, often simply a fragmented absence of knowledge, seeks a return to the Self. And the laws of the dimension in which we live will bring someone into our lives to help us to see it. This harbinger of conflict, is actually a key piece into healing our own souls, if we can open enough to realize it.

It's the separated psychic energy that opens a door of access to lower energy. And the person we find conflict with, is actually carrying the fragment of our soul that we are missing. Fragmentation sets up a psychic vacuum for the return of our energy. And it is up to us, as to how to retrieve it.

While I have had my share of conflict in a life, when I reached an age to understand that a life change was in order, I chose the less chaotic path of introspection. And for me, *that* involved contemplation, journaling, occasional fasting and many vision quests.

When we consciously step out of the conflict in our world, via internal work of some nature, we will then be faced with that same conflict within us. This of course being the reason most people choose to stay busy, to avoid this awareness. And that is because, at least in Western Cultures, we usually aren't given the tools for a remedy, to heal what we find. We usually are not even taught about the concept of spiritual purification.

While this book is beyond the scope of developing the particular skills for healing one's soul, (See my book *Daring to Dream* for specifics on spiritual healing tools) it is important to realize the implications of a wound. And that these wounds open us up to the lower frequencies of the Earth, allowing chaos and conflict to enter our lives. This prevents us from maintaining consciousness and separates us from the memory of the highly spiritual experiences we encountered as children, and that we are still a part of in alternate dimensions.

Every time our soul runs into a stressful conflict that we are not able to emotionally handle, the body tenses and a fragment of our soul escapes. The end result is that on some level, we know we are less able to manage and cope with life. We do not have all of our faculties with us. The next natural step, is to become busier, to help us to become less aware of ourselves and what has been lost.

On the astral plane, this means another fragment is sent out into the unconscious Universe, in an attempt to resolve the feelings of discomfort. In some ways, this is a positive result, a God given way for us to experience more in the same space of time. But we *are* dividing our presence among many different existences, hence the result that we lose consciousness in the physical realm.

While our fragments are busy elsewhere, our body is given the space it needs to cope with the current physical happenings. We have however suffered a loss of power, as a portion of our power has been delegated to another realm. But a spiritual practice can help us to speed up the return process.

Through contemplation for example, we are able to pick up glimpses of struggle and resistance, opening a door that might usher this fragment back sooner than later. For when our test has been completed, and everything learned that created the initial loss in the first place, the fragment easily returns home. We experience this as a deeper sense of wholeness that might arrive while journaling, when experiencing nature in a profound setting, or maybe in a simple and quiet moment while taking a bite of a delicious meal. We suddenly just have a deeper sense of wholeness, as if our power just dramatically increased. It did.

The healing of these wounds close the access to the lower frequency energies. If we are humble and aware of our faults, there is no force in the Universe attempting to show us our shortcomings. And I do understand that many people are quite content living their lives under these adverse conditions.

I personally need to maintain a conscious connection to these inspirational realms to feel alive and whole. Others may substitute this for an adrenaline rush. But without a regular connection to the hope that exists in the higher reaches of the Universe, I am unable to maintain my own internal peace and live in a balanced state of satisfaction.

What frightens many people, is this lack of knowledge—that darkness can actually protect us, if we do not resist it. It can prevent us from attempting to receive something before it is the appropriate time. In this way, it can be thought of as much of an ally as the light, if we are able to keep the proper perspective. While it may not be our friend, it can only harm us when we attempt to push through a barrier that we are not prepared to pass.

If it has the power to stop you, consider taking that time to understand its power, its purpose in the current situation and how it is limiting you. When enough light has entered your own body, through prayer and contemplation, the barrier that was once in your way is no longer able to be found.

Sleep Paralysis

Currently one of the most discussed topics related to dreaming, sleep paralysis is also one of the least understood. The Mystic's doorway into the higher worlds, the paralysis state can become a treasured experience once understood and the physical body is properly prepared to receive its intense vibrational forces.

The experience is simply the result of quickening, the body tuning into receive the intense vibrations of heavenly realms. For some, a state of complete bliss – and for others, sheer terror. So how does one person resonate with the experience, while others resist? It's about vibrational resonance.

If the dreamer has completed the spiritual purification work necessary for entrance into the higher realms, before these intense energies are directed upon us in the dream state, every cell in the body will vibrate in oneness with the Universe. There will be no resistance and the result is that a direct path of communication is established with one's higher power.

But if there are too many lower energies within the body, or specifically spiritual wounds that prevent our being from vibrating with the higher worlds, severe discomfort results. What is experienced can be something as simple as discomfort and suppression, to feelings of restraint and doom, or much worse. The darker aspect of paralysis can result in enough resistance to open doors to lower worlds, where demonic forces can arise and enter our personal space. Some dreamers report sensations of being paralyzed, unable to move while seeing horrific visions.

Why does this phenomenon occur?

Regardless if we are having a light filled experience or a traumatic one, there is great purpose in such an event. In many cases, our guides and spiritual teachers have decided it is time for us to feel the pull of awakening, to attain more consciousness in our lives. The result is that consciousness is directed upon us from the heavenly realms. These nudges toward a higher life, even if experienced negatively, still lead us to becoming more aware of ourselves. A negative experience most definitely shows us that there is darkness within, as without that corresponding darkness inside, darker forces outside of us would not be able to manifest in such close proximity.

Imagine a glass of water, how you can tap the rim with a spoon sending shockwaves throughout. Concentric circles of vibration can be seen forming on the surface as all of the molecules vibrate in harmony with the wave created by the tapping. Every molecule participates...

Now let us drop something denser than water into the cup, perhaps an ice cube that floats just beneath the surface. Now when we tap the rim, the vibrations are disrupted. Instead of the water's surface vibrating in harmony, waves are bouncing off the cube. The ice is unable to vibrate at the same frequency as the water. This of course, is the analogy for what occurs when darkness is within us. Untruths, fear, wounds – all resist the vibrations of the higher world's energy descending upon us. And this can result in an uncomfortable sleep paralysis, turning a potentially mystical experience into a torturous one.

As discussed in earlier chapters, the darkness can have many sources. We may carry wounds from past lives that exist only in our subconscious minds, resulting in unconscious PTSD that we have carried into our current physical life. Or they might also be from recent experiences in the current life. In some cases, they have been severed so well that they no longer physically make an impact on us. Even so, they still reside in our light body and will remain with us till released, even following us into future lives. This energy is what can prevent us from blissfully enjoying sleep paralysis.

So how does one remedy this, to become more resonant with these vibrations?

The answers are found in any work that helps us to change our own vibration. Eastern philosophies teach many spiritual practices – simply think in terms of sound and vibration. Massage, chiropractic, reiki, drumming, and sound healing are all practices to change the vibration of the body. They do this by helping unconscious fear, stored in body, vibrate loose and rise to the surface where it can be released. There are many other healing modalities, like entering a personal vision quest, participating in a sweat lodge, dreamwork, contemplation and journaling. Writing in particular induces consciousness.

You may have experienced, in this mystical state (or even a hazy dream) light being sent into your body from the heavens. (The only difference between the paralysis state and a hazy vision, being the amount of consciousness directed into you.) This is yet another way that the coarser energies in our bodies are broken up to free us. The light interacts with the darkness within, transmuting its energy so that it may be released. *Our allies in spirit are often working on us unconsciously in order to awaken our vision.*

But all of these modalities have one thing in common, in that they break down the coarser molecules in the light body, into finer ones. This resulting purification allows the soul to enter higher spaces in the ethers where vibrations are much smoother. When one's spiritual vibration can become smooth enough to enter these higher realms, one is then truly gifted with celestial visions.

Developing a spiritual practice, a daily routine of activity that stimulates and grows our awareness during our waking hours, change the vibrational frequency of the body and simply make us more resonant with these frequencies. The result is that this seemingly traumatic paralysis state, returns to its original purpose – to act as a corridor into the higher realms of life and experience. And what we might find there, is far more grand than words could ever describe.

Psychosis and Spirituality

I believe that on some level, most people have an innate sense of desiring to more deeply connect with the spiritual realms. And it's often completely unconscious. We are just not able to remember what it was like before birth, how oneness was much more easily experienced, and how knowledge can be realized in an instant.

So when born into the physical dimension, we can still unconsciously desire to experience life in the same way. The difference in the physical dimension of course, is that we must now exist in a world of dramatically increased density. The actual molecules of creation are coarser and the finer frequencies of Love are not as easily discerned. This presents a problem, for when we open in the same way, it is easier to absorb lower frequency energies. We have to learn a new set of rules in order to find protection. And those arrive in our life, through experience.

As I have already suggested, lower frequency energies are detained near the Earth. And when I say, near the Earth, I am not necessarily talking about physical space, but instead frequency—the dimensions that vibrate in frequency close to the vibrational frequency of the Earth. And in the multiple layers of thought surrounding our planet, exist many entities that lack experience and knowledge. These entities can pose a great difficulty for those diagnosed with or experiencing the symptoms of psychosis.

There are dangers in opening to the internal worlds before spiritual purification is complete. Spiritual purification removes lower frequency thoughts and beliefs from our being. Deepest desperation, frustration, and aggression are only vibrational matches for entities that haven't yet learned to receive the inspiration and hope of the higher realms. Darker, unpurified emotions within our being can open a door to under evolved entities and invite them into our personal space.

So there is good reason for the majority of the population losing consciousness of the dream worlds. And that's so they are given time to cope with the demands of the Earth, and to unconsciously begin the path to spiritual purification. For when that purification is complete, the inspirational frequencies can find a home in the hearts of those that have released the bonds of the Earth, even while they remain incarnated here.

But there is a great temptation to return to those worlds before it is time. And this can result in symptoms of psychosis.

While I believe that psychosis can be induced by many different means, including experiencing a severely traumatic event, the need to return to the consciousness we knew before our incarnation can also act as a door.

I don't want to claim that I am an expert on psychosis because I am not. There are many that devote their entire lives to its study. But I can speak to this in some degree, because during the first stages of my awakening, I was severely harassed by lower entities.

Many in the medical field still believe that the symptoms experienced by psychotic patients are hallucinations. But even Jesus spoke of being tempted by lower entities as a part of his trials. And this is perhaps something that all aspirants must endure, as a part of the initiation required leading up to spiritual awakening.

During the awakening process, you may find that there are entities that might arrive in your life, willing to instruct and guide you every step of the way. *I always treat these entities with caution.* It does become more obvious who these are, later on. Those aligned with higher God power will want you to develop your *own* power. They know this can only be done through the correct use of your own intuitive heart. You are not developing power if someone is telling you every action to take.

Lower forces make promises—God delivers.

Now there have been times when benevolent beings have given me warnings about getting involved in certain situations, or encouraged me in a specific action. But again, I would suggest that any being that has every answer for you, is not a benevolent being, but one that is merely looking out only for his or her own best interest. And that's not any different than someone that might wish to take advantage of you in the physical.

But when our physical purification is not yet complete, and we open ourselves up to spiritual dimensions, we can be vulnerable to engage and enmesh with lower entities and experience what some call, *psychosis*.

The Internal Worlds

I sometimes hear friends discussing a great disdain for the life situations in which they find themselves. Perhaps they want to be around more spiritual people or need the world to become more spiritually advanced. I can certainly sympathize with such feelings. But in my own life experience, I have learned to see from a higher perspective—to seek a higher vantage point, above the chaos of mainstream life. While this does not solve all of my problems, it does leave me with a greater sense of satisfaction in my daily life. And in turn, I am gifted with opportunities presented to me in the dream worlds to experience utopic settings. I realize this to be a great blessing.

But if I were to share a piece of knowledge about what I have learned, it would be to share a sense of what it feels like in those realms, where I am offered a sense of expression I can't truly even imagine when I am awake. When in spirit, I can look inside of myself and see the entire Universe within, experiencing a peace that cannot currently be expressed in the physical.

Often in my travels, I interact with the unconscious fragments people incarnated in the physical world, some actually in my life. And in my exchanges, they are usually not weighed down by the same degree of ego. This makes them much more open to hear my words, and to more deeply accept me.

The value of this, is that it gifts me with a greater sense of satisfaction and also patience. Because I can see that people are learning to be more open, honest and compassionate. And I know this will eventually trickle down to their physical bodies when they are awake.

Because I know these new teachings will arrive in the physical Earth, and that other souls are going through similar learning, I can be more accepting of the chaos currently in the physical dimension. I can see that the world is changing.

I know this has to be much more difficult for others that are unable to experience what I am describing, to understand, and know for themselves it to be true. Without seeing this first hand, it is then easy to get frustrated with the world, to resist it and perhaps even demand that it change. Of course this type of thinking is a very low vibration to experience, and so if I could, I would gift everyone with the patience to trust in God and to know that things are really well in hand.

A very important point to know is that we will do far more in the internal worlds—infinitely more—than one could ever do in a single physical life. Deeply understanding this, we realize that if we simply live a calm and balanced life in the physical, however simple, we really make a huge contribution to the world. Our existence in a multi-dimensional realm allows this, simply by living impeccably when awake. So it's very important to live a balanced life here, satisfied with every detail. This enables us to do much more powerful work in the inner worlds, where life is actually created.

Get life straight in the internal worlds first, without reaching in the physical. Then our physical lives becomes easier to manage, as we learn to receive in a balanced way. When we learn to maintain a spiritual perspective, we can be given much guidance, even if only perceived intuitively. We are always being helped, so try to stay in a place that is open to receive.

The challenge comes each day as life's pressure bear down upon us, with the sun grounding us in the physical Earth. Too often this pressure grounds us in the *illusion* of the Earth as well, and not the physical Earth itself. A daily spiritual practice, described and outlined in my other books, can offer us a gentle reminder—to remain above the illusion. Being grounded in in God's reality, even in a miniscule degree, allow us many freedoms.

In my early twenties, I once saw a documentary about a nursing home. One of the residents, an elderly man, had an attitude that I found stunning. Still being immersed in youth, with naivety and very little consciousness, I normally would not have even noticed this man. But somehow I found his words to be riveting and they became forever etched into my memory.

He discussed the element of *satisfaction*. And watching him interact with other residents in the retirement home in which he lived, it was clear to see that he was living a very satisfying life.

Participating in all of the activities offered, there was no doubt this man was special and knew something that many never find. But he said it was up to us to make the best situation out of what we are given. We could be happy or miserable. And here, under conditions that some might find distasteful, he was living a blissful life.

I believe it is possible to find a deep acceptance of every situation. And if a situation is truly uncomfortable, our satisfaction gives us reprieve, opening a door in the Universe for something better to arrive. We can make ourselves happy or discontent…

Karmic Law

Presence, affords us the opportunity to make choices based upon what exists within our feeling body. That in turn, gives us access to many different avenues of knowledge.

Anytime we react, we have the opportunity to create energetic imbalances in and around our aura, accruing a very subtle karma. The Universe is not waiting to punish, but only responds to what we are creating. So there are many forms and degrees of karma. It is not only created by malicious intent. We reap what we sow.

For example, if someone is in need of a gift, a gift that we comfortably have the ability to give, but we withhold. We are creating a vacuum of energy that must eventually be balanced.

I am not talking about giving when we do not have the energy or means to do so. We are not required by the Universe to deplete our stores of energy. Giving to exhaustion creates a different kind of energetic imbalance in our aura, which also must return to balance.

But the Universe asks to allow energy to flow through us. It keeps us connected to our creator. As the life force flows through our being, it connects us to each other, the world and greater Universe.

Many people in the Earth, are simply just trying to avoid taking on major karma, while avoiding participating in malicious action. But what I am describing is the more subtle aspect of karma. And understanding this and the balance that results from following spiritual law, allow us to become more aware of the higher realms. When we learn to balance the subtle energies that flow back and forth from all those that are in our life, whether they are in our physical presence or not, we experience the protection of being One with the Universe.

Sun and Moon

The sun and moon — allies of action in the physical world. Most people do not even realize the impact these great energies have on our psyches, souls, and life choices. While one leads us inward, the other directs us externally, encouraging us to act in the outer world.

These energies regulate our being and guide us in our Earthly life, secretly withholding ancient knowledge until we are ready to listen. But as each day passes, we become a little more conducive to receive the wisdom, as we gradually awaken from slumber.

If we are seeking, knowledge gently trickles toward us. And spiritual guides know the importance of not overwhelming souls incarnated into dark dimensions.

The first time I recall being awakened in the night by spirit, I gained consciousness while coming out of a deep sleep, to find a guide tickling my back with a spirit feather. Instead of instantly moving, I just lay there for a moment to try and grasp what was actually happening. I could see (with my third eye) and feel a feather tickling the center of my back. But the feather had the ability to penetrate my skin—it was tickling me *below* my skin.

The instant I moved, it was over. My vision evaporated as I continued to gain consciousness and I was left just slightly amazed. Then I remembered an important dream. The guides wanted me to awaken in this instant, in order to remember...

I had begun to intuit that it was good to wake in the night, to help the dream memories resonate in my being and allow them to shift my consciousness. And so on occasion, I would get up to journal for a few moments.

But then one night shortly after falling asleep, I gently began to re-awaken and noticed that I could see light coming through my closed eye lids. Opening my eyes, I discovered a guide had actually turned on the light in the room!

A few years later, I came upon an article claiming that our ancestors didn't actually have a single sleep cycle as most do today. They had *two* sleeps and would awaken in the middle of the night for a lengthy bit of time. Some would even get up to do things, read, and probably spend a little time letting go of the prior day.

After reading about this, and then contemplating my guides regular prodding to awaken in the night, I reconsidered my sleep patterns. While I have not adopted a two sleep cycle, I make note of the enhanced power of contemplation during the middle of the night.

A female guide once whispered to me after waking, as I considered getting up to journal, "The sweet fragrance of the night."

There was more to her communication than words, as her energy revealed a sense of the magic provided by the night and what it offers to the seeker.

We are simply able to access the greatest depth in the internal world, during the middle of the night, when the sun is on the opposite side of the planet. We may also be able to contemplate similar issues during the day, but our discoveries will be on a more elevated level and contain different aspects to the same issues. Physically grounded by the sun energy in the daytime, we see from a different viewpoint. But the greatest depth is easiest to come to us, in the night.

And the deeper you go into yourself, the more healing you can receive.

When we can find and receive the stillness of life, we breathe in the breath of God. Our greatest spiritual allies can draw near and more deeply influence us, even if only on the unconscious plane. Be busy and remain scattered, we diminish our presence and lower forces are allowed closer, affecting our choices.

Boundaries

During my first vision quest, I stood up for a moment and wandered a few feet from my circle before taking a seat on fallen tree. A few moments later, an armadillo walked up to me. With the spiritual vibrations, or *medicine*, of the animals still being a relatively new concept to me, I was anxious to read about the armadillo's vibration. As soon as he walked away, I quickly grabbed the medicine cards book I had brought with me.

It told me that the spiritual teaching that the armadillo brings is about boundaries, learning the proper boundaries in relationships, in order to be able to interact with people—without having to accept their limitations.

This quickly hit home, as I was having a very difficult time discerning between what I wanted, and what mainstream believed I should have.

Anytime we receive or invite a person into our lives, we also open ourselves up to the spirit allies supporting that individual. Choose wisely, as the unconscious influence of those around our associates, can be more confusing than the people themselves.

Perfect your boundaries, and love can easily come much closer. Darkness is kept at bay. Maintain a state of worry, thinking about what you do not want to have in your life, and only darkness can enter. The state of tiredness that results can open your aura to receive all kinds of lusts that breed discontentment and confusion. Unconscious rage can build and again, a door to the lower worlds opened.

Feeling despondent often means that conflicted energies have been given entrance into our aura. Other people's thoughts, once entering our energetic space, can then appear to be our own. And they may be in great conflict with what we want for ourselves. The result can be that our own internal guidance is in challenge, and that can bring depression.

We are only angered by darkness and become willing to fight it, if we are afraid its message is true. For if we know, deep in our hearts that a message is false, we remain at peace.

For those that have opened a door to the internal worlds, it is a loss of boundaries allows lower entities to gain entrance. There, they may say something to frighten you, while pretending to be your ally. God gives knowledge through deeper awareness, and realization. Peace and calm is the result of receiving divine wisdom. If it is scary, it is not from God.

The Gift of Wholeness

I have certainly lived a very active life in the physical realm. I've done some of the most exciting things possible – I've been an avid scuba diver, ski jumped, trained race horses, flown airplanes, and more.

But when you are able to wake up in an out of body or lucid dream experience, when your consciousness and wholeness has increased twenty times or more than in the waking state, suddenly you no longer need the same kind of excitement in your physical life. In fact, the simplest activities can become deeply satisfying, as we re-learn how to see through the eyes of a child.

We may attempt to put what is outside of us, inside, in the effort to feel whole. (By keeping our main focus in the external world.) But the energy we find outside of us in the physical realm, is often chaotic, and the result can be that we actually feel *more* fractured and unstable. It is very difficult to build consciousness, when our unconscious action is lowering our vibration.

When the chaos outside of us has entered our being, we then become enmeshed with it, in a battle that cannot be won. The only solution is to remove it, through divine connection that results from working our spiritual practice.

At some point, we can become grateful for psychic attack, as it is a needed reminder that we are not whole, that we still have something to heal.

Holding onto something, we leave God's protection and lose important aspects of our being. Holding the dense matter in the Earth, we are grounded to its frequency. And in that state, God is not able to come closer, to advise, warn, and guide. Wholeness must wait for our release—for *us* to release.

A Higher Purpose…

Imagine yourself, still in spirit and prior to an incarnation. For most of us, that means having a greatly diminished sense of ego. It does still exist to some degree for most, but without the density of Earth, we have a dramatically increased capacity to feel love and oneness with our surroundings. Why choose to leave?

For some, there is no choice. They must return by karmic obligation, but the purpose for our incarnation is the same. We purify the atoms in our body, in our being. And that delicately, or dramatically, reduces the density of our personal egos, opening us up to receive greater wisdom when returning to our home in spirit.

Final Thoughts

I would like to suggest that the mainstream consciousness in our world, remains bound in conflict with its darker aspects. Most of us try, in almost every way possible, to keep darkness at arm's length. We really don't want it anywhere near us, and particularly not within ourselves.

But there is a point when we tire of trying to find a balance when standing squarely at the end of a spectrum (where balance is not possible), that we desire to give in, to receive. Our willingness might be assisted by failing health, or perhaps resistance from those around us or by our own spiritual seeking. It is these moments or through these experiences, that enables light to enter. When we are cleansed of our resistance to these lower fragments of our consciousness, we may realize darkness can be our ally. We can then allow our shadow to return home.

I can spend a life waging war within myself. I can even *believe* I have won. But what happens to the aspects within me that lost? Is it really possible to divorce myself from any darkness within? Or do those aspects simply remain in hiding, as lost pieces of a fragmented soul. (Where they are still unconsciously expressed.)

Loneliness is simply the awareness of one's soul being fragmented. When we are feeling lonely, we are remembering that part of our soul is unable to reside peacefully inside of our body. And the resulting lack of wholeness leaves us pining for *our* return.

I am both light and dark. And the soulfully rich moments in life that I experience are moments when I am deeply accepting all of the pieces of my soul—when I am able to feel all of my feelings without reserve.

When I can experience life, at least to a degree in the same way as when I am not incarnated, I am bringing my heavenly life—down to Earth.

Do not feel lonely, the entire universe is inside you.

Rumi

Recommended Reading:

The New Mediumship, by Grace Cooke. Available at Amazon.com

Cultivating the Divine, Healing the Dark Masculine, by John Stone. Available on Amazon.com

Gifts from Above, How Spirit heals us during Illness, by John Stone. Available at Amazon.com

To learn more about Dreaming and the author's Retreat
And Summer Camp in New Mexico, visit his website at
www.consciousdreaming.org

About the Book

A veteran of thousands of out of body experiences and visions, John Stone shares his knowledge of the spiritual realms in *The Spiritual Life*. After learning to traverse the internal dimensions and facing its challenges, Stone teaches us about the tests faced when opening up to experience the greater Universe.

"At some point in our evolution, when we desire a deeper connection to the Universe and a Higher Power, we will face lower entities which are simply seeking Oneness with us. For until we can face the darkness within and learn to manage the unconscious expression of it, dark forces will always be attracted to us."

This book is about learning to understand the forces of attraction and repulsion in the Universe and in particular, how to neutralize lower forces in our inner lives, as well as in our daily physical life. 'By gradually becoming conscious of ourselves in the internal realms, we learn a new appreciation for those still mired in desperation. And in doing so, we are freed from the psychic attack that we could potentially otherwise attract.'

About the Author

For the last two decades, John Stone has been sharing his spiritual discoveries through his writing, books, workshops and personal teaching. Today his work continues to evolve and can be easily found online in blogs, websites and social networks.

He spends his spare time writing, and teaching out of body travel and psychic protection, while enjoying friends and nature in his mountain home in the high desert of New Mexico.

Visit John Stone's website at www.consciousdreaming.org to discover more about dreaming or to make plans to visit the author's retreat for Dreamwork. Dream Summer Camp begins soon!

Notes

Made in the USA
Charleston, SC
04 October 2016